ROSES IN THE RAIN

BY

QUENTIN WILLOWBY

ROSES IN THE RAIN

Copyright © 2021

QUENTIN WILLOWBY

PUBLISHED BY

GOORAGANG PUBLICATIONS
ABN 77 845 063 813

to those who know our planet needs protections now

The author was born in southeastern Melbourne in the early thirties and matriculated from Melbourne Boys High to the University of Melbourne from which he graduated MB BS in 1956. He became a rural GP until 1969 when he went to the London Tavistock Clinic for specialist training.

He wrote poetry because 'it was there' and was persuaded to collect it in the seventies. Melbourne So Far Away, was published in 1981. He required a pseudonym.

He received encouragement from many people including senior poets. From the internet he was no longer QB, but Quentin Willowby. That was okay, then belatedly found that Melbourne So Far Away had been accepted into AustLit for some time. The second collection Motley Leaves, was published in 2017.

Poems that have been published elsewhere.

Two poems 'Swifts' and 'Lyrebirds' in the 'Birds' section, first appeared in 'Motley Leaves'.
Gooragang Publications 2017. ISBN 978-0-9386836-1-6.

'Haircut' and 'We' appeared in 'Melbourne so far away'.
Christmas Creek Publications 1981. ISBN 0 949741 00 0.

The poem 'Pigdons Place' was first published in 'Zen is development' in Section Development IX., as was 'She knows there is nothing else' from section VIII.
Tamarind Publications 1996. ISBN 0 9586836 0 3.

Authors acknowledgements:

To Marg and Pauline for their feedback and editorial intuition, let alone their detective work.

Of the unnamed artist who is producer of the setting of both 'Motley' and 'Roses'.

To Ed Wright who challenges my horizons.

The Department of Pacific Studies ANU who have written significant historical background and developed my interest and respect for many cultures who faced being overwhelmed by European Intrusion/Invasion.

To those who know Australia is a Pacific country.

To those who can see the stresses and cultural disruptions brought about by homo sapiens on a planetary scale.

They also see what it does to nearly all the other species: extinct or eaten.

i

Section one: Introduction

The Death of Freda

... renewed my covenant with trees,
pulled kikuyu
to the point of pain;
spasm spreads the message
that some stubborn self endures.

Later with Armagnac
from a Swedish glass balloon,
warming liquid lens refracting deeper gleam
in high lit arcs of circlet gold.

Face-warmth spirals to the chest,
soaks to finger tips
who stop their play,
still the tendrils of the pain.

Uppsala Cathedral

Disbelief?

But I am glad.
Glad of freedom from beings outside the cosmos,
outside life,
pleased that such disbelief
is the basis of my knowing.
The Oneness of All That Is,
and my own self
an ever-changing part thereof.

The full awareness needs some quiet
away from vaulted roofs:
the sky is wide and makes no traps,
yet here is contemplation
of the pale grey stones,
the gentle greens,
the special quality of light
imparted to the tapestry,
the central cross,
the silver fingers spun,
the light so sown
to feel the peace among the Oneness:
    light and man and stone.

Introduction

Spectator   *25/3/20*

While the genus homo
loses many species and itself —
such chances to survive:
blow away, day by day
purple pain to watch
in midst of cosmic shock:
a globe fouled whole
    while you look:

Every nerve in its place
blood cells for their special role,
cone-cells in your eye,
are all together to survive,
yet plague-like populations drive
beyond the limit
    of their lives.

When its 'mooring' broke
ice-mountain floats on sullied seas
soon afternoon. albedo lost;
phyto-plankton's light went off —
no hint of turning orange first:
Palm-oil remains, a taste for beef,
North tundra melting fast —
methane, and See Oh Too
    for breath.

Then the final top —
Asia misses an early stop:
Bush meat sold again?
the virus cloud abounds,
older lungs quickly killed —
    dying still every day.

Changeless voters too,
pet 'Pollies' go their way
"Doesn't matter"
Jobson Tax:
obsessed with coal and gas,
fixed by their distraction
in the middle of the fall,
while wonder of the neurone net,
as more of it is known:
unfunded perils still not shaped,
yet thickhead jeopardy
    maintained.

The Biped Plague

Hermits and the moon in Leo;
the ebb-tide stays a lonely moment,
sucking when the crabs are running,
beads and incense lost in sand,

found and lost the way of power,
comb the beach for humans trusting,
take them and their rules and reasons,
foci of their social ravings,

foundations in the dunes above you,
civilise with laws and mores,
burn the ti-tree and the sword-grass;
love their hopes because you need them,

bow to whim and strength of power,
ways of living,
lines to breathe by,
'who fucks who' and 'who shits where'.

That is what you're crushed by,
when you build a road to somewhere,
and, in utter desperation,
be with others where the road ends,

join their legion, form a culture,
be a termite working blindly,
lose the heated mating on the beach,
weak and helpless, overpowered,
fettered by the master culture,
spawning falsely — ignoring nature,
planet plague now a feature:
sullied seas, spinning storms,
the only home of every species,
losing now the One Blue Pearl.

Haircut   (1975)

perhaps
the way i sat
but the eyes were hers
kind like yours
relaxed
living

and yet those eyes are mine
a man's
unafraid
of crying bedlam and cold stern men

I know it for clear memory of face
brought to mind
in the barber's mirror
which haunts me gently for a moment
gently
without pain
quiet to go
and come again

Fate   (2016)

As the divine wind
wrecked Kublai's fleet;
and the stung foot shout
of the thistle rout,
Rescue left 'The Cooper':
Bourke and Wills —
a few hours out.

Cinema made 'The sliding door'
needed as a metaphor;
smaller here, but recognised,
fate-bites find us anyway
old humans face them day on day,
more beings join – more doors slide
morseled fate, the world obeyed.

To balance these unheralded life changes, when we must
keep going, I want to tell about Leigh Sales recent book 'Any
Ordinary Day'.
I found it comprehensively valuable.
With empathic respect she has been immersed in the 'feeling
storm'/ what next/survival of those struck by fate. More, the
value at each level, is for all who must suddenly adapt to the
unexpected.

The endorphins of contentment

'Not wanting' is rewarding:
the outgoing loving of others is easy.

The body functions as is its nature;
harmony and good feelings
are the usual experience.

The endorphins of contentment
are more reliable than any
from the poppy or test-tube,
and, once experienced,

would be difficult
to return,
rebuild
the imagined attributes
and wants of 'I'.

Section two: Birds

Assault bird *(gymnorhina tibicin)*

The black backed magpie calls in ire
at other life to leave his range
and dives at head
with beak and shit
to back up doubt what he's about.

The boy
nonchalant of face
left hand on his handlebar
copter cyclist smiles
bike-pump rotates above his head.

Feathered missile shrieks his run,
aborts in time,
foiled in shock
yet take another try —

success —
his foe has gone.

Birds

Jacky *(dacelo novoginae)* 'Kookaburra' In Australian

London Zoo   *Regent's Park October 1969*

"Hullo Jacky!
Oo – oo -oo! C'mon Jacky!
They don't even know your name:
'Laughing Kingfisher' it says;
But you're not laughing now —"

Here, shapeless leaves fall in death,
the sun shines dimly in the South;
the family chorus long way gone:
the faux tucker's surely wrong.

Your beak, my fingers, feel the stringy-bark,
crush young leaves and smell them true.
"Jacky! Laugh for me — Laugh — or I'll cry.
Laugh at all the pommies passing by."
A calm but cheeky, brighter eye,
tail lifting to the sky,
feathers ruffling on your neck:
this is how we're meant to be —
          Free!

Bellbird gully *(manorina melanophrs)*

...sweet descant chuckle
explains
thirty-nine-month old's speech
"Ava just said, 'Grandpa's hair is like white spaghetti.'"
bing We all laugh
Even me. *Bing   bing bing*

Ava beams around the room
Happy families **bing ding b-bing**
Three layers of **bing** life around her
Four, or more counting **them** —
We are **bing ding** guests of these green birds
you only hear   you never see
until you know them well,
quietly coming to a plant saucer
for a drink.

Some days back home
I found that comb.

Birds

Azure Kingfisher *(ceyx azurous)*

Blithe bird
who burrows
in the bank to nest
bound in beauty
to the lowest branch
reflected by the pool.

Patient, quiet,
following unwary fish
with clearer eye,
then perfect dive —
control of space.

While machine maker
self-destructs:
superior conceit
within the scheme
of changing life,
denies this bird
its prior place.

Lyrebird *(menura novaehollandae)*

To hold a glade
own the mulch beneath the ferns,
damp disintegrating logs
decaying on the forest floor
hurried with segmented life,
the lyrebird mimics calls of species
that defend their ground;
yet his *'clip of axe'*
and *'surge of diesel'*
are ignored.

QUENTIN WILLOWBY

Birds

Red — The Canyon top: Kauai Hawaii *(paroaria coronata)*

This cardinal
had a mate
quietly dressed
who waited
for the visitors
to leave.
Their forbears
flew from a cage
and survived
despite the fact
that he was red.

at Princeville
and at Waimea
the Russians
built a fort
at either end
of Kauai.
and stayed
over a decade
until a king
required them to leave —
an Alaska irony.

An exiled German Jew
told the fate
of lowly peoples.
His telling
became a cause itself:
a push against 'the-haves'
from 'the have-nots'.

16

Birds

Had he not,
and had not the tide of blood
at its flood
taken The Winter Palace,
a Romanov
may have stood high above
Waimea Canyon
feeding sugared bread
to a red bird.

Birds

Swifts *(apus pacificus)*

In Summer,
             insects tapping panes;
From high branches
   gum-leaves breath their rustle/roar
         in a dry wind

Who revels in the rise
before the nimbus band –
updraft of the storm-cells edge,
flies before the rolling front?

High swifts
   in easy flight;

their space-dance falls into the year.

Here could be my totem; 'Swift'.

      To fly low   the
                         In   hot
         folds
            of
               air   with food
                        thick

possess spacetime?

Who knows where?
Or that freedom encompasses the orb
because a Sinkiang cliff-ledge leads to this storm front
that bends our Woodville trees?

      Kindship, spirit,
the symbol flies triumphant
      life on life on life
         renewed.

Section three: Tiare Tahiti

Tiare Tahiti

As if her own name
she insisted
I say it clear

Ti – a – Ri   *(tee ah Ree)*
there are three
sounds to be
sung by me

She put the pure white star
above my left ear
and warmly laughed

> "Here are we
> small flowers
> delicate as the scent
> and easily bruised
> if put aside."

Tiare Tahiti

Papaya and a squeeze of lime

Gentle Huahine rain upon the thatch
papaya and a squeeze of lime
take the Fare path once more
they've strung three stands of wire
before her grave
some lettering renewed in black
the baby's name —
and then Elizabeth Ann
and words picked out below
to indicate to those behind the wire
she was a missionary herself —
as she surely was;
and in Tahitian at the base —
mourning and respect.

Tiare Tahiti

First days in Tahiti   *Le Truck 1974*

Hail it here?
Anywhere?
This will do.

bend
to scuffle forwards through brown legs
student   (from her books)
smiles shyly   sit beside her
across   a mother quietly tickling
young boy on her lap
older woman   rubs her nose
gold and warm
faces dignified and graceful
their eyes as bright
and warm as sunrise
brown as mulga when its polished
beside the mother   young girl
shyly thinks   of something other
bouncing
as 'Le Truck' is bumping

          driver
bulk of man   taro fed
great arm waves
oncoming trucks of colour
blue and green and yellow
his children   boy and girl
warm and happy
playing in the cab beside him
tyres and engine roar with freedom
vibrant   daring
trees and flowers
      acceleration

Tiare Tahiti

across my shoulder
lift my eyes
to hold Moorea as horizon
looping   lurching corners
rushing stream   women walking
held excitement
Gauguin's people   Gauguin's colours

on the left   lagoon   greens and blues
boats and palm trees
turn and wheel with the corners:
shudders   bumping wildly
mist on mountain
more Moorea
Passing in the centre lane
Be-eeep! **Barp!**
pieton   smiling   waves to driver
laughing   engines revving

to a stop in Papeete,
two leagues from Puna'auia:
Granddame smiles   Tarif twenty francs
bids us part   shyly   warmly

Tiare Tahiti

The Marae Stone

On a small marae
in Oponohu valley
is a stone placed for Ta'aroa
many centuries ago.

It shared mana
through the toes and heels of countless Chiefs
and chants of power of the priests.

It held new people when they came
with strength of paddle, sure of song,
looked to Oro
sea and wind, rain and sun,

until the year of eighteen-nine,
gaunt men from London sailed into the bay,
brought urgent tales, a magic book,
money, measles and 'The cough':
more potent sacrifice:
the god himself modelled true:
"Put your body on 'The Cross of Life',
then The Kingdom waits beyond."

Soon those who then remained,
left the valley for the shore and sand
and made obeisance to the cross of wood,
embraced the ideal parent from the sky.
The stone is covered with the finest green,
living moss, a vital sheen;
and through a corner of the stones
a giant chestnut, strong has grown
to join cathedral canopy above,
and two expanding chestnut roots
have gripped the stone,
to lift it clear above the base.

Tiare Tahiti

These stones have often been returned
across the oceans, many years,
by those 'too late', 'who did not know'.

On a not too distant day
one loyal to his separate god
might forget the stone of life,
its place of rest,
and deliver it away
where fire-forged crystals fall,
are taken by the rain
into the earth,
the reef, and then the world.

While One is young,
so many leaves have gone.

Tiare Tahiti

View from Puna'auia. *(late afternoon looking northwest)*

As the line of ocean, lifts to the sun,
pays in liquid gold towards us,
comes without pause,
my pulse beats
towards some inner light.

To the left towards Paea —
blue and clean, white along the reef;
to the right, stark Moorea,
hibiscus sky behind
fades to peach bloom,
the light goes on in glory —
change -- simple story,
round as the Tahitian moon —
Darkside seen in Earthlight.

Tiare Tahiti

Toerahu, The North Wind   Maeva Huahine

Canes flung among the flying leaves,
the fibres torn, flailing thatch departs;
Manura-of-the-long-canoe
was brought no gifts upon the wind
thrown helpless in the heart of Tane.

Such power to supplicate?
Or when war-canoes appear
then Oro,
god of peace and war appease
or fall to fear.

Then ships and cannon:
many parts of power
descended from uncoloured seas —
The Fathers came   the people waned
Which god to be?

Tiare Tahiti

Mururoa Atoll: *Nuclear testing 1966 - 1996*

A sign from Oro;
the blood cloud clots
upon the spine of Raiatea
to green and gold
as Tane fades
the war fires light.

Ta'aroa seems to hide;
only with the dawn
might Tane make vahines smile
and babies dribble milk.

but Oro —
blast and fire at Mururoa
poison fungus to the sky,
and later, in the quiet fall
of Strontium to the soils:
the food, the milk,
and all those lives
the gods had built
poisoned in the bone
to live in fear — ?

Section four: Earlier Poems

Earlier Poems

Chapel Street Prahran Vic. *1950 this is the earliest Ms*

... walk on
my figure alone
breaks the soft silhouette
of foul dank shops
whose line fades
through the haze
and never stops
as step follows step
on block and stone.

2019 comment. It was a cheerful party for the birthday of one of my
Jewish friends, but as a gentile with no girlfriend, I was aware that I
didn't fit in too well. Late in the Melbourne night I was walking to the
no 7 Tram-stop to catch the hourly all-night tram. This business area
collapsed in the Great Depression and had not recovered after WW2.
I was 16.

The Basilica of St Mary Major   *Rome September 1969*

I looked at both, then to myself to say,
"Where is this God to Whom man prays?"
Above, I looked at The Inca's gold:
"Not enough for all the ceiling," we were told.

Across the floor a clear face came;
Her walk awry, her vital body lame,
She listened, smiled a little now and then,
brown eyes down the columned nave.

I thought, "What greater than her mind
has arisen from our Universe?"
You might say, "That man two-thousand years ago... "
but others too, minds who'd sow
a seed to grow to justice;
man, no longer owned by other men,
now schooled to thought at younger age;

she thinks then... for herself, as He did too:
she is not blind; her eyes are open wide:
no pattern stamped upon her brain.
"Stolen!" she said. The Inca's loss, Isabella's gain.
Golden guilt above. For all who see, to see.

.... wanted a hundred lire too,
to shine the light on Moses' face.

Earlier Poems

Stories   *Darwin 1975*

Life is full of stories,
half finished,
some resolved.
And when one's own
seems tired and stale
and will of living melts
or feels the same,
another set will bring
the monsoon front,
the rising of the blood
across the opal sea.

We'll gather in some days
and take the road;
we'll see again the Timor Sea;
flying soon we'll see Moorea
or grand Étoile
will spin us through the years.

Other lives will brush the pollen of their stories
even sad or droll,
some living with us now.
Seems at naught without a story
and another story can't be bought
but just be told;
now so tumbled, no beginning'
no real story to unfold —
don't want any special story
and the last one
locked in sadness,
must be carried here alone.

Scribbled words encourage
the very spirit now on hold,
make some doubtful hope arrive —
There will be changes,
patterns — broken —
thick now and uncertain:
    no lit-up path to see.

Share the space among the trees   *(1981)*

Flying friends
from many homes,
folios of many styles,
small goose, a duck life lives,
or honey drawn from special blooms.
Rosella wars: dead stump close by,
three kingfishers with different lives:
one laughs to mark his place;
Azure skims the line of creek,
and the Sacred now in Borneo;
The snipes are in Japan: swifts — a cliff in Sinkiang,
and a drongo - more than a pub mate's curse.

The Protestant child: Mid-20th Century   (1987)

You — the ideal:
porous children strive,
and again, when grown;
they try to live as sheep
not goats
as The Word might say
and, so accepted —
No other way?
Not for You the Oneness of it all.
With no chance — guilt remains.

    Guilt - so easy won
    Guilt - to overwhelm
    Guilt - to drive the gears of great endeavor
    Guilt - to stop the body juice
    Guilt - to paralyse
    Guilt - to be the bonds of life
        tossed upon the cart
        on the dreary narrow way.

Without a choice, you see it long:
only friends with hard pulled smiles,
nothing really close,
not free to feel   body touch,
distance is the norm
each path alone
'salvation named'— and no one won.
... and all the other dross that may remain
can lose the hoped-for fantasy —
        'Developed You'

Compulsive games are what are left:
'Goodies and Baddies'
the classic one in many forms.

But look out—
subtle power named
   'What you did not do.'

So what remains? —
   a skin-tight, bound-down pawn?

     Inside —
the blood and shit
     of many fears
     that man and woman
     might contain.

Earlier Poems

Ferns and faces   November 1962   *written 1972*

Memories of the mulberry tree,
of little children laughing in the bath;
the fire built up in early morning
looking to the coloured quiet outside.

But the fear inside
denied by pride —
had not died.

Door bell ringing,
jangling phone,
imperative morning,
sickening, mad;
dark noise inside,
loud and strident

'Daid!" she cried "Mar-Io daid!
Confusion, fear, divided, breaking:
"Look out"
they said.

Driving fast,
gums and grass tufts by the road
potatoes, the red soil ploughed;
"Look out for Mum, she's mad."

"Dead', I said.
Bedlam, Babel, blows about the head;
motor revving, driving faster,
ferns and faces fixed forever.

The cedar and the mulberry yet grow strong
and many trees have grown,
and more will grow;
the wind will play the camphor-laurel
as freshly as Australian snow
lay beneath the other tree
on a cold June morning
before life moved on.

Nuclear preoccupation   *1979*

Early in 79 there was a rise in nuclear distrust of the Soviet Union that later
stimulated formal agreement. That level of nuclear anxiety did not appear
again, until the latter years of the twenty-teens.

The news decayed —
repeated stories of the early strikes:
The four we took ourselves
self-portraits broke in pain
Humpty-Doo after North West Cape,
Sydney still survived;
Confusion wrought with static and white-faced voices —

Four; No more!
The predictions so trite and true,
that a great rage burnt me
at the old-old-men of death-too-soon,
whose fire eclipsed the petty battle
in the Canaan Hills, or Ragnarök —
the Northern skies inverted
with such a band of lethal dust
that hope not burnt by flame
or neutrons through the bone,
faced a cold unkind
that never was foretold.

There had been others in the Southern arc:
Island bases and at Simon's Town;
steel shapes beneath the sea
blew the great and small away:
So — clustered to the radio,
we heard the counts, the moves —

From Cairns they took the highway south
from Darwin through the sky;
for the UV bane we now prepared,
as, when minutes saw a cloud recede
the November sun was strange:
the light was leached and painful to the eyes.

We drew the curtains, dropped the blinds
and watched the eerie glow through darkened glass indoors.
At night we worked, dressed the quince
in garish plastic, built a lean-to on the Emperor mandarin,
shaded in the fowl house,
but preserved the bins of grain.

Yet the work continued with the day
I opened the large umbrella
and painted it thickly with white paint.
It smelt of thinners:
but soon dried, and droll — strange figure
gloves and goggles carrying a white umbrella,
dressing the apple tree in jeans
and a voluminous yellow mu-mu.

Strange how sweet were tears
and soft water from the tank:
early we'd blocked the downpipes
with panty hose,
and sealed them with some tubes of goo.

So, the invisible violet burnt the grass,
the maple curled and dried by noon;
and retreated by exhaustion
to a darkened room,
we heard the warnings sounded:
overcalm expressions of our fate.

Earlier Poems

In those days we did not know,
assumed some thousand fireballs
and countless millions
dead of blast, but by Christmas
the truer story came:
dust layered the stratosphere:
The Northern half had formed a cloud
so dense, the missing ozone triad
In our upper air — a minor mark
upon their demi-world of always night.

Three billion froze they said,
another billion burnt and blinded by the bane
without the knowledge of the darkened glass
or thought to husband seeds, reserve the food
before the Winter yet to come.

So, August now, we are not blind.
Smiles and flanks are thinner
In the easy circle of my arm.
The Winter cold defended by
the stack of wheat and coal —
exports to 'however',
nowhere in the North, never to be known;

cough a little, shuffle feet,
wake heavy in the morning
watch all the stranger clouds,
And thankful that the sun
when it returns, at least is pure,

but 'The Alice cloud' spread wide:
rampant cells to kill the blind,
or fighting off surviving crews.
The Cold, the lonely isolation
of our placement in the void
broke our frame and our resolve.

Yet the ozone layer renewed,
Strange, my fear, it peaks today
after so much we survived.
Now primitive, not rads or rays.
Will Maitland echo Capetown? —
to the might of lead and steel?
Once more the right of impulse,
wars of tribes;
we could die —
for want of law.

Earlier Poems

Christmas Day Mood   *Woodville NSW 1982*

The cool water matted my body hair
but soon evaporated
leaving a forest trap
for the tiny winged insects
who struggled – tickled their way —
caught their wings
until I lifted them out
and dropped them into flight
above the mat.

I'd brought the cattle back to
the first twenty,
enticed them through 'the Queensland gate' with hay;
the grass on the hill crunched in dry death,
the air tasted of dust and dung:
and my hat stayed on
when the sun was almost gone.

The mosquitos whine at the screen,
moths tap against the glass:
there is hope here at Christmas time
that the days will shorten,
the sun will have more mercy
and there will be some chance of rain.

Those who are not carting water,
can talk of other years crops,
how this drought is 'longer'.
Some might forgive impatience
at the images from The North:
we have no feed for reindeer
and suet puddings with brandy-sauce
invite only polythene holly.

I can look at the casuarina I cut last Thursday
decorated with stars and tiny dolls,
and feel joy that another circle on the way has joined,
and that beneath the tree
are symbols of the bounty of our life.

When you look past the she-oak,
I can see 'The baby' in the stock-trough
surrounded by distractions,
yet the symbol of our annual renewal,
creates the space-time of our year,
to live safe and fruitful journeys:
and care for every child we know:
                not remembered
                    by our teeth.

            ****

Stories of Sigi *(venerable dachshund 1958 – 72)*   *(1989)*

Pointed oak leaves
    oranging
holding their twigs
sheltering many small glans
gripping their sap supply
through Winter into early Spring

like my stories of Sigi
that Cassie would listen to
repeated over ... and over
But —
telling of her
to 'A wise four-year-old'
who said:

"Cassie isn't real.
Your imagination Daddy.
Like Googa!" (her imaginary friend)
A short-arm jab
at the bridge between the eyes;
wonder, salt-tears,
the beginning of a belly-laugh —
together:
yet the sum was sad.

I still wanted somebody to whom
they were both real ...
Malcolm perhaps ... to take over,
tell it now
while I found the pin-oak tree,
hand to bark,
the digging holes,
possums, cricket with a plastic ball,
when he was young —
a darkened Melbourne afternoon,
an elsewhen safe
from losses.

Section five: Changing Millennia

The Insult

Bird Storm of The Holy River
when she was nearly four —
sudden — she met me
at the downstairs door:

shopping expedition made us four,
In chaos wanted my attention —
Shouted —
her insult to succeed—
     "Peanuthead poohball":
laughed hilariously.

... Immediately amazed:
alliteration not the least —
five consonant syllables — two feet
so balanced and distinct,
graphic neologism so blunt,
Saxon bite, diction straight.
Perhaps there is a gene,
or spirit of the talk
that no one taught;

Changing Millennia

The Woolly Cloud ... difficult enough for the adults

the woolly cloud seen up front,
still it with a gaze;
hold it as a finer taste of self —
extended in the sky:
from ragged window way up high;
observe
the world of 'Ground' is 'Up'
and fantasy returns —
confused and frightened child:

Only one from a multitude.
Who me!   Why me?
Necrotic breath of beasts,
to cage the wayward
In their teeth.
Blue and baleful biosphere:
banehole in a young child's mind
creeps out to test the air.

Every crag alive,
streams of green digestive juice;
greasy hair
drops a little blood upon the touch
excrescence of a naked brain,
and oil-slick lights,
fly across the purple sky.

The beginning?   Yes.
Testing, also:
culture, rooms of peers,
responsibility,
long years at school, formal and for everyday,
saleable self becomes
now trained
in a crazy waring world.

Changing Millennia

Have said it long:
Here: blunt and short:
rescued notebook page:
loopy longhand - lost file found.

Or mark this writing strange —
mystic words from eastern worlds
sometime to accept;
relay to Western word:
Everything that is - as One - divine.

And even from divisive mind
every God described has meaning:
see Mystic Three in One;
yet, loss of ideal parent
in 'The Other Place' —
despair:
and take defense within their skin:
called by others Atheists,
or struggle --
in irresolvable vein:
call themselves Agnostic,
social raincheck,
or choice between delusion
and perception of the blind?

Is the culture kind?
The skin defense is not as safe:
the bald and brutal world
does its way,

Changing Millennia

Friends and siblings,
the valued working life
hold together?
Always more to come,
roles to fill:
flexing fearless words,
basket forms a cradle,
new thinking is allowed
until   amazed in view
of what the human self can do.

Changing Millennia

November 4   2020   4.07 pm in East Australia

Night cold takes Washington
Crowd and police mill about each other —
"Still don't know
Rama return?
Or Mahatma required?"

Loss .... Confusion
The leaderless
on hundreds of respirators
defeated in six figure mauls,
unawake death
while his ego still blooms,
not horror reviewed.

As the ocean heats up
Blue planet
Distilled.

Changing Millennia

Herself

... is all alive:
consistent —
every star
   process,
      probability,
         energy:
as silver atoms less can do,
when an iron atom moves,
its fields come too.

Look through The Milky Way
in The Lord Howe Sky,
when the moon's left home
'All This' you'll see anew.

'All This' is really 'Thissing':
our brain does thissing very well,
and the thissing of Everything
is Herself
and occasionally
there are some such opportunities —
where You know Yourself as well

This week new space-walk,
solar-cell repairs;
no-gravity felt
by distaff hands
yet orbits earth in hours.

Changing Millennia

Their neurons outnumber
The Southern Sky,
cell connections more —
than when galaxies collide.
Their brains a greater marvel,
can stay in space a while —
mend a cell outside.

A baby learns to speak:
outstrips our friendly astronauts:
Force always was 'M' times 'A':
Energy: mass 'C' squared:
a bounty
when consistency is All.

But catechist rules compete,
take up fighting, save their might:
then all the words that start with 'd'
beset not only kingdoms,
but the home of many species,
when we can not agree.

Dualist fantasy:
cannot bear Herself —
wishes Her away.

From inside, eyes are open:
awesome sense of wonder — small eternal we.

Section six: Songs

Malcolm' 1959

"Is Malcolm on the beach today,
warm sand washed from toes at play,
blue eyes watching for your smile:
he'll give you that seaweed in a while?"

"Or is he nowhere — somewhere here or there,
down among the yellow leaves drifting through the air,
or friendly with a pigeon in Trafalgar Square,
lost among the gum trees, looking up the track,
riding in a lift, or walking down the stair,
listening for your footsteps,
when you come back?"

Songs

black apple dreaming: *Four peoples came as one*   7/11/19

'The reef' is still bleaching,
tomorrow its gone.
A glacier is melting
the Ganges will slow;
the tundra is thawing —
California in flame:
please reassure us
we can stop it in time?

Woolgoolga Woolgoolga   Woolgoolga she said
Woolgoolga Woolgoolga   Woolgoolga she said
Woolgoolga Woolgoolga   Woolgoolga she said

The trees are all withered
the cows have no food
The Darling's dry bed
the fish dead and gone,
the East Coast is covered
in smoke haze too soon.
What can you tell me
to light up my home?

Woolgoolga Woolgoolga   Woolgoolga she said
Woolgoolga Woolgoolga   Woolgoolga she said
Woolgoolga Woolgoolga   Woolgoolga she said

Songs

New desert is forming
so light is the rain;
Main Street is closing,
the retailers gone,
the coal-train's still rolling
always on time.
What can you tell me?
when Scomo says "Fine."

Woolgoolga Woolgoolga   Woolgoolga she said

Woolgoolga Woolgoolga

Woolgoolga she said

Woolgoolga Woolgoolga

Wool gool ga

She said

Songs

Umbrella song   1971

"J'ai besoin de un parapluie.
"... pluie, ma Cherie, aujourd'hui".
You turned away, Dear, away from me.
I'll hide my cheek now so you can't see.
"J'ai besoin de un parapluie."

"J'ai besoin de un parapluie."
The lightning flickers crazily;
We've grown apart Dear — you and me
It's too late now — as you can see.
"J'ai besoin de un parapluie."

Songs

Which Bubby? 1973

Which bubby saw the waves boom over?
Which bubby had her toes in sand?
(and sun and fine gold spinning softly)
Who laughed across the table?
Who held Mummy's hand?
Who spat all her cereal outside?
Who shrieked in glee at moving leaves?
Who slept so soundly on my shoulder?
Who's loved so much by you and me?

Songs

Moving through the traffic   Austin 1800

Moving through the traffic, I like to swing along;
a dance it seems, a rhythm, breaking into song -
the lights are green, we get away, fast change to third,
wheels are spinning underneath, the thrill I get's absurd.

Early in the evening, when most are going home,
in mind I drive a power launch, belching creamy foam;
along Victoria I drive against the horde,
and foot against the board, I pass a lumbering Ford.

A little mist across the bridge, a downhill run,
motor purring smoothly, today this life is fun;
'Skipping-girl' is with me, soon we will pass,
our lights greet gaily — "much longer this can last?"

Driving in the city, with the bright lights of night,
when wheels and seat are part of me, this deep delight,
flows sure for me along the shine of silver line;
the cars, the lights, the pavement, all of these are mine.

Flight song   1974

Over and over, over we go
Over the clover in squares down below
Hither and thither, wither you go
Cover a lover whose dear heart I know

Down we go under, and over we go
Under the thunder, loud the winds blow
Lover and lover, together they go
Wings in the sunlight and shadows on snow.

Songs

'Getting younger' song   1996

It is easier for an old man
not to win the race,
they who have their selves to prove
will more enjoy the chase.

    Ref.

Getting younger   Getting younger
the way that we might be;
the less we make our mind up,
there more that we can see.

It is easier for an old man
to crawl upon the floor,
with dolls and block-built towers,
himself is shared by all.

It is easier for an old man
watching women walking by,
they help him to remember
he knows the way so well.

It is easy for an old man
to be humble and be brave,
or an old man to be quiet
with the world's way so near.

On Verse (xii)

Look out for poems that sing the world —
There are many 'round you on the air:
"melting in the dark', or he 'is leaving' —
or denouement of the powerful play.

... create the trees you walk among,
starting place to trace your dream
or here to brood in echoes
of the tongue so flung to set your mood.

Perhaps some have space for you
to follow with a singing of your own?
Whenever —
you and I ... are not alone.

Songs

The lettered score   On verse (xiii)

The measure of verse is like music
but short and long, rise and fall;
it might sing beside the spoken words
yet each reader takes his poem
    from the lettered score

It is of melody of spoken speech
and grows from gracious lilt and form
of those who speak before the market door;
or, from tradition's valued page
    may ring Elizabethan stage.

Do rising words take rhythm from
    the inner ear?

Or sounds gather to a frame
    of stirring beat?

When stanzas take to voice
from either side of evening fire,
then base guitar so amplified,
or griping vibes from careless speech
    might break the rhythm ....
        In our reach.

Section seven: Travels

Travels

Exercise for French teacher

"Savoir, autrefois
ce que'on sait
aujourd-hui."

Un paradoxe,
une vision
des hiers
sans deuil,
flottant sur
le bord
argent
des reves.

Renoncez – y
et agissez
maintenant.

Threads   *Journey to Troms June 1983*

Tomorrow the threads unravel
to make a loop of life;
we do not go to Seattle
but swing around the world.
The loop will be in space
climbing the latitudes
in the Narvik train,
crossing the long lines in a bus
when we know
night will not come.

In loops,
the threads cross again
compulsively they cross,
draw all directions to the knot
... not empty void,
but immanent in
mass/energy spacetime — Knowing I am a process —
but not substantial like a bit of gravel —
still brings me peace to ride the loops of karma —
even a process aware of process,
has a wealth of places in spacetime.

Travels

Contrast

Sickening contrast
quietly proof-reading
poem: Traveller

I'm not sure
Scottish sheep
dozen or so
lived on Mull shore when at home,
or the other side, Iona

They were coming on our boat:
midsummer grass growing fast.
The shepherd kept them —
wait their turn
find their place.

A quarter hour on the water
Bright of eye
to jump out at crossings end.

****

The New Book:
Pastoral care for sheep
a metaphor
for the tending of our fellows

The Old Book: Genesis 1: 26
God gives man dominion over all the animals.
****

Intrusive horror
gasping sheep, nauseous head
rolling in a swill of dung
dying — days of tortured heat

Tight packing shippers,
(********) by name,
claim a better time of year
to cross 'The Line'.

Packed dehydration in tropic sun;
shit and carcass own the floor,
panting tongues, legs fold under,
we humans bring abuse/neglect

for dollar numbers paid
to suit some family
in The Middle East
to kill their own:

ignorance and venal frame
beside such drawn out death;
The Middle East from Perth —
stretched out alien horror,
one we cannot own,

Big Business defended 'strong':
"The grazier's right to sell his sheep."
"There is a good time of year
to cross the Equator."
and "The economy '
has rights too."

post script: 29/5/2020 A large animal carrier docked at Perth has staff taken off for Corona virus infection and the ship cannot leave immediately. Fifty-thousand sheep are waiting in yards nearby to be transported to the middle East.. (source ABC)

Travels

Melbourne to Narvik: many rails were laid.

I shall sing of him that boy
who shouts out "Burn-a-wee"
the window seat he kneels upon,
anticipates the cut of view —
'East Richmond' is the call.

Where is the boy
who watched the lights,
knew all the points,
touched track in respect,
went all the way
to Gembrook
Puffing's Billy's soot in hair?

..... or travelled overnight:
slow Sunraysia express
through red dirt
and orange trees;
Murray River heard his song:
the fears he found.

Inside the Arctic Circle
took the train at Bøde
riding South to Trondheim
standing at the rear
where the track
would twist and curve behind,
some stations, many a bridge,
summer petals
        flying in the wake.

Again, in Norway —
the joy of boys is found
In miles and miles of track,
across the Arctic circle,
around the fjords edge,
or further by the rivers
or through the tunnel's maw —
 the pleasures of a train.

On some tracks near Oslo
you can sit beside the cab:
a view beside the driver
looks at the track ahead
The lights are green
the crossings flash
The platforms passing by —
a viaduct, a rushing stream,
or watching all the points.

The fun of being young throughout, an easy fate to bear;
 while some men are growing old
 the wiser ride in trains.

Travels

Cassie and bear go to Europe   1976

Ted Ted with the earless head
Went to Sweden and went to bed

Ted Ted went to Norway
Met a girl in a doorway

Ted Ted in Luzern
Found he had a lot to learn

Ted Ted went to Denmark
Met an old man from Renmark

Cassie then was almost four
Ted looked more like sixty-four

New York   1983

In a cool May wind
light leaves of locust
take the sun.
The view from a forty-first floor
of their Lady of Freedom
holding up her lamp
five or six miles to the South;
breaking blue rock under blankets
at Fifty Second Street;
or the pushcarts,
hot dogs,
kebabs and ketchup
taste anew.

Nudging taxis
under-pavement rumbling
ravages of stress,
the walking tired,
aggressive voices being right,
the old Polish butcher
whose sermon in the cab
is inspired by the poet
Wojtyla.
Handsome faces —
black with the confidence
their looks deserved
and tears for many.

Suddenly
Entering Fifth Avenue;
cleaves confusion,
abrupt and serried colours —
pastiche of passion
crying to be whole.

The ancient Hue pagoda

... comes a preserved child
looking through new and old lenses
focused finely in parallel wonder:

The child is found:
Jesus' koan understood
(climbing younger);
nature action dances simple theme
as Jesus' *bhikkhus* formed anew
at the beginning of 'The way'.

'Seeing/knowing'
hard to share
yet could be found
in the Hue pagoda —
gong note:
not of sermon
or from book.

Identity:
photons from the morning star,
sound waves in the Viet air,
gong or sun or distant star:
they are all and everywhere.
Integration: as the son of Eric saw.

Yet the body wants to run:
lift, engage, write and teach:
as an active male in his latter teens
ignores the age of bones;
the breath is right
so much action there to do,
nothing but the wind
holds karma's horses waiting for release.

Chao-chou's model I am sure —
an uncertain thought,
(lateral lapse perhaps)
abates as clearer view
bundles the eternal fire.

Section eight: Viewpoint

Viewpoint

Argentine soldier *Falklands war*

... waits endless weeks:
misty breakers beckon,
beg the rifle barrel
to disrupt sea music.
Maudlin conscript soldier
wishes even Fearless to his cove.

"Oh tobacco! Oh tobacco!"
Black smoke columned
from a crumpled wing,
and chocolate parachutes to sea?
Grey British shapes along the waves —
or shedding sky?

The dawn arrives,
yet no one comes.

"Let us go find gull's eggs,"
wander on the green hills.
dream now of the pampas:
firelight, beer and girls.

When the landing came —
    ghurkhas.

Viewpoint

St Hilda at The Styx

The rock and dust were there
without the thought 'rock' and 'dust',
and shades of shape without the light.

Some part of waking then prevailed
orienting to the lack of pain
and the vanished tubes and wires.

This dream could thus be 'death',
loose dream to leave the hurt behind —
the toes and face mean nothing now.

"Judgement!   I am soon to pay my due.
Something soon – I still expect..."
But then she heard the water by her feet.

And when the figure loomed to being
her lips shaped, "St Peter is a joke."
... and then she found a thought in fear:

"Dear Jesus!   Please! Jesus is the one."
The figure straightened; a mist upon his face,
one hand upon his boat, the other palm upturned.

She thought of gypsies, knew him not,
and cried, entreated, shook and railed,
then knew at last. "Money? Money Here?"
"I have no sin upon me. My husband was the one."
The figure waved the empty palm, raised forwards,
then pointed at the world.

"Go. Go where?" She didn't know.
He sat and dipped an oar without a splash
and thoughts were gone and so was pain.

The boat was further from the shore;
she turned, and knew she must yet search
   ... and search again.

    ... tubes and wires returned.
    "You awake?" Claus said.
    She coughed: peered at his face.
    "It's only you." Coughed again;
    "Bad dream," she murmured.

Viewpoint

Entropy and Gravity

In Winter by the fire
'Now' extends in such a way
everything extant - becomes

Summer?
the thought —
The Universe will simplify,
disorganise, cool off,
hammered
by The Second Law,
pins to board
the philosophy of who we are —
Apocalypse
in stellar style,
and all who Summer makes
have their end.

Thermodynamics: Isaac N.
Such the view of Entropy

To balance:
Isaac A, coined the word 'gravitics';

falling off your bike —
you know it well,
the proverb too: 'must come down'.
Yet not so well, the shape of space,
and shaped to pull mass to mass —
our blue Earth formed this way
to grow and bloom in our life today.

Many mysteries of the cosmos yet to see,
so,
don't bend low to Entropy.

Jim

He flew
threw himself through
escarpments
peak to peak
torrents touched to laugh
settled
pushed his chin left high
In the coloured words
   sideways
       indeed sideways
vision of flight impinged
on enclosed rooms where here we stay.

"I'll show you reality! ..."
Fist to shatter glass

mind flew through in freedom wise —
thoughts not made
by social dross
or pruned by two thousand years
of Aristotle's hold
upon a culture's frontal fold.

He let go
safe enough to ride
the storm of thought:
to know that down below
we'd stand there sure,
admire him in our way
and keep our thoughts
in lines and rows
and bow to those of verb
strait-think
gravity and walls.

Viewpoint

The needle gate

Intuition
   history
      speak as one,
they are swift to draw
the sword and fire the gun.

Sometime
   they were
      Greeks and slaves:
defeat of death,
the tender warmth of Him
was not so left
to children or the meek:
the needle gate is stuffed
   with camel hair
      and swords of praying knaves.

Their issues
   are so straight
many a place to lay their head,
mothers yet to be interred'
the right
   are very very right;
   the evil are possessed:
   chaff or goat,
   marked to pass beyond our sight.

'God's soldier'
   unsure,
      anxious of his vision blurred
         turns about,
           you see a gun —
           run!

We

Open mouths Xuan Loc,
blue rose lips
spittle nearly dry,
limbs are not yet stiff
— asphyxiation
Michigan made.

desultory rockets
fly into Saigon — singly.
The people wait;
the people gather
to talk the war
single-mindedly to a close.
Will guns . . .
accept only justice.

They who went to fight
were requested four weeks later;
we feared the wingless dragon,
burnt his shadow
while he laughed.
We believed politicians:
power There was power Here:
many young ones died.

We . . .
blustered badly,
Ming vase broken,
forfeit honor
      sadly shamed.

Viewpoint

The stone in the river   (1969)

Other — over there   the lip is moist

You're on your own   No boy. No Mum now. Step the right way.

Which way?

This way

Which way?

You are still standing on the stone

I can't. Better to live on a stone than drown in the weeds

Enough tears will make the river flood, but that's no way to Hope.

I can't swim

Yes you can. You're windy

I won't

You never would

Shut Up!

The water's warm

Like Hell it is,

Try it

84

I did   It's cold and fast

You can't stay there Rick

No I can't. Can I?

Still there?

Smart aren't you?

Not really

I'm frightened and you won't help

> *No, I'm not even here and anyway; it's me of twenty*
> *years ago so I can't help.*
> *You're lucky I'm even in your head to talk to you.*

Lucky! Hell

Still there?

It didn't deserve an answer, they'll start shooting soon.

About bloody time

God knows what will happen, but I'll be off this bloody stone.

Viewpoint

... she knows there is nothing else

to have a religion   is a tree necessary?
a fig tree particularly?   symbol or shade
communication or throne?   a figure centre stage?
a male lead?   form once more
firewood or doorstop?

a buddha does not sit under a tree
she spreads her leaves to her light
she flowers
she is scented music and moonlight

when she is called a buddha
for the want of a better label
it misleads
there is no buddha

she is not a buddha
because she has practiced zazen for many years
she is zazen itself

she is not a buddha because she is silent
she is silent to avoid confusion

not a buddha because of effort
at an obstacle she is energy

she laughs at negation

she is not a buddha
because she has drawn now and timelessness together
she knows there is nothing else
when she hears talk of a buddha
she goes on with her work

she does not seek emptiness
it is her peace and her power

her energy/compassion is like a thunderstorm

her smile engulfs the Orbit of Mars

the reader cannot find her
only experience her

Viewpoint

"... meets the blue-eyed monk"

1   Admission Office

Sawdust still upon his hand,
face gentled by the beard:
Inside he's travelled all the way.

2   Mens Ward

"... you waited for me to wake up.
You... you're not the nurse
who admitted me last night?
I didn't tell ... well —
enough to be admitted.
Why do you look at me?
as if you Know?

You do know,
and yet you just sit there
and treat me like a person
and yet you know.
You know then that I'm afraid?
Yes. The world is strange
and takes a wild and shattered way.

How I've prayed;
He lets me see so clearly:
but I am to be long in the wilderness,
if you read the book,
but the book
is all they look at:
wilderness of words
that stay the same
and nothing grows.

Viewpoint

Who? You are a man?
You smile? I'm a man.
For a moment I thought ...
but Satan is a metaphor.

He who sent me,
hides what is to be:
how many times
I've come this far?
So many hundred years
and I feel more radical
than I have ever been.
I think I am afraid
that this time
they'll not lift their eyes
from 'The Book' for long enough
to know I'm here."

Separate! ? ......

W' ...ell   No

Thank you!   I'm awake."

Viewpoint

Boxing day review 2018   *(retyped 30/1/2019)*

'memberence this year, sickened gut.
Pearl Harbour Day some weeks ago,
or Nikkita stared down by JFK —
blips — by the portents
    of today.

Power can warp the old Greek art,
hold the media, farm the vote:
Idi, Stalin, reappear,
greed among the weapons,
blinder ones have the guns;
home paddocks spread the fear,
not just here and there:
The blue planet
    has them everywhere.

Power press from many shores
built gates and walls, border blocks:
our news today counts many wars,
camps of hopeless loss abound:
in mind, the dead they left behind.
And others are the different ones
who hope to find a kinder land,
simply want a better chance,
improving lives and calmer mind.

But change is fast —
mass of people pushing past,
polluting species,
sullied sea, rising tides:
can't bear the future they have made;
    want
        the old times
            to return?

Viewpoint

Today? The unknown?
Will the Acid Ocean change its way?
Year Twenty-fifty — Food Enough?
Tarif wars?   a world recession?
Nuclear targets
        now aligned'.

Somehow,
they chose a six-year-old
to play potus games at whim.

One hundred years ago
the worst war ceased a month before.

New hope, new rules,
The nations forum — direction found?
New hope (shrug)?
and some of the men were going home.

Today, The Northern Half
is war prepared
in every part.

Guatemalan girl cries beside a border fence.
    wants the land
        of many guns.

Section nine: A gentler speed of living

A gentler speed of living

'a gentler speed of living' *Easter Casino NSW 1975*

How many pennies in a pound?
Six gallons of petrol hand-pumped to the bowl;
Pet pulling a load of Mallee-roots
when the wheel fell off —
slow by Sydney's toil

      Away
Where life flows slow today
Age may have dignity
or be like Uncle Whew

Sitting   this verandah   still
In greens and rain
vivid antigonon
hardly moved by warm drops
falling perpendicular
to join in life   the colour
and the feathered green.

Antigonon-pink holds sway
against the rain   commands the quiet
seemingly the world   the strongest voice
to speak with coloured music on an Easter day

(in memory of Isobel and Garnet Raphael)

A gentler speed of living

Canada musing: silver-birch trees at Tooronga Australia

You peel white bark
around the tree,
Freda's tree
they were all her trees
decorated
with the dancing keys to my memory
like cricket
when called to tea.

The timbre of her voice,
her tighter smile
when she was angry
you would know,
then hear out loud
each clear word
in her special voice.

That was her style
to 'have her say'
and 'have her say' once more.

Canadian spring
has Creswick Street sting:
Ontario birches: Melbourne chill:
her trees here,
grove on grove,
standing still.
She haunts a land
that she hardly saw.

I now stop in the street
and see her trees —
remember her as I please.

A gentler speed of living

Haiku   at burning time

a clear afternoon
at burning time
the family works in gum-smoke

Haiku   the jetty

at the jetty by the quiet water
girl and ducks
share bread and joy

Haiku   early forsythia

early forsythia
fir cones on the grass
a black squirrel ignores me

A gentler speed of living

I live in an age...

I live in an age
when a man called Michael Collins
looked at The Earth coming into view
over the Luna horizon
and telling about it is believed.

I live in an age
where I might print my words
some thousand times
upon the whitened paper,
make the casts of doubt,
laugh at falsehoods,
thumb nose at hallowed lines,
to replace them with a canvas
now safe to know right here.

I live in an age
when eyes still drop
to ancient books
and 'Heaven here'
gets not a look.

I live in an age where
hope for a second life
of holy grace
in a glorious place
still sells apace.

A gentler speed of living

Look past Orion,
through the Milky Way
cosmic glory viewed so wide,
wonders of this life to know:
never separate
is Herself.

Everyday energy are we,
her limbs and thinking,
every being,
every mite of cosmic life
all songs of 'Her'
now and now.

A gentler speed of living

Dicament day

Bird Storm of The Holy River
was almost three,
alone with Granny
on a weekday afternoon,

when she took on
the back gap of Granny's chair
to do it new this time.
Feet, and body followed:

her head had grown;
only her toes got down.
With her walker Grandma came
to the shock and protest yells.

Her head was firmly held.
Granny, cool carrot reassured:
Explained 'predicament'
in gentle tones,

reached her phone
and Liesel was at home.
Ten minutes, she arrived,
lifting comfort, all was saved.

Months later, sitting in a soft framed chair
one-eighty turned,
 from underneath she reassured:
"Not a dicament Granny."

"Jean Piaget overthrown?"

A gentler speed of living

Warmth in the Cold   *Sydney Winter 1973*

... of rain and handknitted woolen socks
prickling warmly on my toes,
rich brown now, then a woolen sock grey:
I've still saved some —

I mourn — with the bookcase
I hadn't seen in four years,
a shirt or two,
green and black striped trunks,
and cold wet windy days
that come to Sydney rarely
out of a Creswick St past.

Cassie is asleep,
Uncle Ludwig plays his eighth;
the river lies like lead,
yachtsmen stay at home
and I stay warm inside
with Alicante in my cheeks,
satisfied with such a day:
a Winter's day at that.

A gentler speed of living

Lessons six and forty-three 1950   On verse (xiv)

Written 2020 The names are authentic except for 'Hotcat'
— Marg had named him Petrovsky

Hotcat bit the rabbit:
  Bun
then ran amok,
Jumped up, leg aloft,
hit Hotcat midships
then ran at him again
as if to hit him quick,
but bit his head instead.

Barney was half Persian,
around before the bunnies came:
lazy in the afternoon,
while Fluffyboy
cauliflower leaves
consumed.
Cruciferous craze
never Barney's thing;
and steak —
hardly the other's dream?

A gentler speed of living

Roses in the rain   *1983*

This time to San Francisco
I laugh with roses in the rain,
Buses   tipped across my window pane.
Feeling for my summer self thirteen years ago,
In sadness when the movements are the same
since I flew West the other way:
first trod this square,
now two moves from that home
to a struggled destiny,
self-questioning of courage
in the knowledge of my will.
My own volition,
whatever journey on a plane,
still laughs with roses in the rain.

Section ten: Australia

Australia

May 1975

The end of the Vietnam War
and re-drafting of The Family Law Act in Australia

... have become history in the same month.
I wonder what will happen
to 'The private Eye'
and 'The Drinker'?
They can wait outside in yesteryear.
One fault alone?
Which bird flew with one wing?

'Seventy-five'
If only to have known
that the cruel war
and family blame
were to step off the train
almost together
to dwell in the living past:
jointly by prayer
for 'freedom' and 'the family'
from the unordained —
and those who died.

There WAS hope:
For a people — IS hope.
May they not go
the way of Sydney trams.

Australia

The other flame nearby

The host exposed:
steady flame
metaphor of life
relit — controlled;
incense at the centre of the skull
draws warmth and power on request
in Sacre-Coeur —
a union
womb inspired.

Or back here: Alcheringa,
The Dreamtime deeper
by ten thousand years —
from Rainbow-serpent holes
Pelican spirit
Jealously shares his food.

Paddle quiet,
take the tide in dusk,
hot coals within the hearthblock
in the bark canoe.
"Blow them red to white;
Feed the flame."
Rays of warmth within the skin
... she feels the fish upon the shell-hooked line,
glance up, one flash of eye,
takes the other flame nearby
dances from the glistening face,
dampened
in the darkness of a smile.

Australia

On the Muloobinba shore
precious fire against the dark
where dead ones lived deprived —
only living men have fire.

Sheltered under rocky ledge,
their ground, their power;
the patient watchers
sing of quiet to little ones,
gaze across the low-scrub shore
at tiny flames in river dance:
        hide, reveal;
        dark, reflect;
        rise and fall;
each
holding slow its place
before the tide at Kooragang,
lines to take the fish
that come and come again
        .... eternity to here?

See it now in Eighty-one:
King St traffic lights ...
a Yamaha accelerates ....

    A people bound
    Their fire was drowned.

Anzac Day Ballad 1963   *The Minyip bunyip coot*
(fulica atra) or (botauris poiciloptilus)

On a track some miles from Minyip
Old Joe, he walked alone,
stumbled on towards Rupanyup —
his boots on crumbled stone;

His mind was fogged, his feet were sore,
that day he'd had a few:
now out of town, far from the law
he'd stopped to see a friendly tree

And camp down for the night.
He sat right down
but did not to see
the water on his right.

With hairy hand,
he wiped his brow,
his back support a root: 'The cove who didn't care a hoot.'

The red gum stood against the sky,
branches held out wide
to catch the breeze and let a sigh
waft to the other side.

The land was flat, the stubble shone,
The moon caught every straw:
Its image in the water moved
closer to the shore,

Australia

Joe, he snored, and surely proved
He'd have to sleep it off,
but something hidden in the reeds
let forth a raucous cough;
Again, it came, a broken croak;
The Minyip-bunyip coot
With a hard note from his throat awoke
The Cove who didn't care a hoot.

Old Joe awoke, but fifty years —
unlived, had not been born,
he had not downed six thousand beers,
and many sheep were not shorn.

The other fellas in his boat,
they must have felt the same:
some timing crux with the oars,
as if their boat was lame.

The Turks were shooting fast and straight
from high above the bay,
between the rocks his bloody mate
flat out beside him lay,

no further — but a broken shout
a blow, and on his feet
he ran towards the cliff to rout
a foe he couldn't beat,

He staggered straight towards the dam,
his boot caught on a root,
The slush received him like a lamb
'The Cove who didn't care a hoot.'

Australia

Cheviot Bay

(the disappearance of the Australian Prime Minister Harold Holt just after noon 17 Dec 1967)

The tranquil silver of a swelling wave,
a warning slap at vanguard rock
the simple seething of the kelp below
and somehow he would know
the undertow was slow.

Welcome pulse, chilling surge,
fresh of greeting, knowing lover,
her deep green pools and flowing sand,
washed around this dreamtime land,
holding forth her lulling hand.

He took the welcome, arms outspread,
she rose roughly, churning sea,
poured and boomed, frothed, attacked....
Only then to know the dragging undertow
deep beside the rocks to flow;
he stopped ....

And as for we, and our ancient land:
he we lost – to the sea.

Maitland to Deutschland

Such a tentative sortie,
albeit the second,
testing the air,
feeling the contempt
of the girl in the bakery,
(Mind you, I said "Drei" and held up two fingers)
then marvelled at the Churchill cigars,
thirty to a box,
forty-two deutschmarks;
but when I pedalled waste
upon the track from The Nord Express —
          that was my Lancaster

In Trier I tried the local wine
and felt like a Norwegian on holiday.
In the restaurant,
the family at the next table
had brought their bright-eyed dog.
He tore up a paper serviette
and we shared admiring smiles.
Yet when Isobel fed him schnitzel on the floor:
a straight Australian crime,
I looked around — a start —
child's reaction to a hundred films:
the arm bands and the boots,
cruel fantasy of power ...

We laughed —
he looked around for more.

Australia

Journey to the Fourteenth floor   *Sydney*

All the pieces fit together;
we with Tao blending,
The Cove to Quay relating,
surging to tomorrow,
such stable time-sweep building of a great and modern city.

Men and women living — higher here to zenith,
the Harbour binding oneness,
with the city holding
     closely
               the greatest of the oceans
          and careless of the wonder
     at the fortune of their joining.

April 2019

... held the future and its past
with that look around the eyes —
Was then, will be,
Was/is,
still finds the longing
and the deeds of love
between we two
are tension in a feeling field
    together tied.

Should seconds come,
one and then another;
life is but a second long:
Absurdity, artifact —
As 'eternity'.
'elsewhen' and 'now'
defense against The Colossus of Existence
not cramped by simple 'sequence time'.

Australia

Razzamatazz

re the planning of a large new shopping
precinct in The Hunter Valley circa 1979

Teach them small,
design the goals,
and call them 'Freedom brand'.
Repeat   Repeat   Repeat
greed is fine
envy is the main design,
aspire to Cargo,
"You're adult!"
Pump them, suck them,
subtle, sure,
pack in eyes —
stuff the sockets rude;
status notch and pulchritude,
battery trained to buy;
take your token to your packaged friend from Channel 12:
cardboard effigy of video,
cheap the chips
to throw away before you queue again;
swallowing - its own reward:
pounds of plastic chewed
and aluminum soon,
hanger Boeing wide,
kitsch culture on the stage inside.
"Join In!
Join In!
You must have fun."
buying reflex,
hearts are won.

Australia

"They choose it anyway." they say.
"We only plug the brand.
Scientists haven't proved a thing."
Yet — Fill the questionnaire on our packaged self-esteem:
"Be with it — UpToDate!"

Volume and the colour —
    ideal marigold

Australia

Pigdon's place. *(Christmas Hills)*

Sitting on close cropped grass,
there are many sheep tracks,
and, to the right, rabbit dung
on a small scraped mound.

Breath is quiet;
Winter sunshine is absorbed,
air is fresh,
a light breeze cools an ear.
Without thought
The Eternal Face is heard.
It has form and is formless,
has no form
and is not formless.

> *The nature of the way is such*
> *whether you say many words*
> *or are silent,*
> *If you see*
> *or have the comfort of the blind,*
> *have attained or failed,*
> *anonymous or found,*
> *empty of illusion,*
> *or counting The Ten Thousand Things.*

The Timeless Self holds it gently in The Hand,
enjoys breathing.

Australia

To reach a century

    ... prevail,
symbolise the years
by running between wickets
when willow-arm impels the ball:
it skims the sward,
spreads the gulls,
divides the guard,
clicks the wood —
bails go to ground.

Score and chance and partner plays:
mastery of little life
stroking to the long-off fence,
but hazard of 'the outside edge',
and brown hands sure
inures to — **'Out'** — the finger rise.

further clichés then appear

The Murray Valley after Many Years   *May 1968*

for Jo, Mal and Doug

The river does not look as wide,
the hunger is a void long gone;
the time of lonely words in rhyme
from boy inside of man will climb
to life beside this life of mine.

And here, no longer lone, it finds
a crowd, some seed has come to fruit
I look with wonder and relief:
with louder shouts of life
they jump and play on a latter day.

The glass is turned forever down:
yet here, some other peach trees bloom;
the gordos, still on either side
lilies on the river ride —
every red-gum leaf ...
renewed.

Nomad N22B

As the wheels roll past
on 'zero six'
vibrating box with planing wings,
mundane and firm,
until I see down there
with unattached
earth-bound eye,
doodled plan
set with lights,
glowing lines to draw
with progress
on the patterned land
suddenly unreal —

'Where' denied —
yet by modern magic sealed.

Australia

Dreamers

Smoke across the river ... the Rickarbys
were dreamers:
dreams dispersed
in wind across the gully,
like the ringing of the axe bite,
echoes join the next stroke
yet fade to quiet
among the leaves and hills.

They had their dreamtime – dream place
Christmas Hills   hot and dusty, cold and dewy —
dreamed above 'The Glen':
wreathed in smoke drift,   cloud or dust fold,
prey to fire,   full of stories,
like an old man's smoky beard
on a damp and colder morning.

We were dreaming near the hilltop,
watched the evening train come creeping,
watched the smoke-trail cross the bridges,
saw the moon   light silver candles
on the mountains to the North

Yes, we're dreaming, true to dreaming:
found the bush before the Hippies,
found the journey without shooting:
not at Mafeking,
Seoul or Mekong,
not Passchendaele or Dunkirk.

Australia

We didn't choose them;
were and can be dreamers;
such peacetime comes from looking,
seeing in the distance —
the distance found within you.

Yet the other side died in Flanders,
battle at Polygon Wood:
Master's mate at Trafalgar:
the destroyer close to Cairo
but, like the others,   crossed the ocean —
wooden ships,   wind and sails: —

both sides had a lot to give then.